P9-DMH-963

FOR:

ay the Lord make your love increase and
overflow for each other.

1 Thessalonians 3:12

FROM: _____

Promises of Love for a Woman of Faith
Copyright 2000 by New Life Clinics
ISBN 0-310-98249-9

WOMEN OF FAITH

Requests for information should be addressed to:
    Inspirio, the Gift Group of Zondervan
    Grand Rapids, Michigan 49530

Assistant editor: Molly C. Detweiler
Project editor: Sarah Hupp
Editorial Assistant: Heidi Carvella

Printed in China

01 02 03 04 05/HK/6 5 4 3 2

PROMISES OF LOVE

FOR A WOMAN OF FAITH

inspirio

The gift group of Zondervan

PROMISES OF LOVE FOR A WOMAN OF FAITH

ON

A Love That
Perseveres

The LORD says:
"I have loved you with an everlasting love;
I have drawn you with loving-kindness."

Jeremiah 31:3

❧

"With everlasting kindness
    I will have compassion on you,"
    says the LORD your Redeemer.

Isaiah 54:8

$\mathcal{L}$ove always protects, always trusts, always hopes, always perseveres.

1 Corinthians 13:7

❧

$\mathcal{C}$ast your cares on the Lord
and he will sustain you;
he will never let the righteous fall.

Psalm 55:22

You, O LORD, will keep in perfect peace
   him whose mind is steadfast,
   because he trusts in you.

Isaiah 26:3

❧

We know and rely on the love God has for us.

1 John 4:16

❧

Show the wonder of your great love, O LORD,
   you who save by your right hand
   those who take refuge in you from their foes.

Psalm 17:7

$\mathcal{L}$et us fix our eyes on Jesus, the author and perfecter of our faith, who for the joy set before him endured the cross, scorning its shame, and sat down at the right hand of the throne of God. Consider him who endured such opposition from sinful men, so that you will not grow weary and lose heart.

Hebrews 12:2–3

When you pass through the waters,
    I will be with you;
and when you pass through the rivers,
    they will not sweep over you.
When you walk through the fire,
    you will not be burned;
    the flames will not set you ablaze.
For I am the LORD, your God,
    the Holy One of Israel, your Savior. . . .
You are precious and honored in my sight.

Isaiah 43:2–4

The eyes of the LORD range throughout the earth to strengthen those whose hearts are fully committed to him.

2 Chronicles 16:9

❧

The eyes of the Lord are on the righteous and his ears are attentive to their prayer.

1 Peter 3:12

❧

From everlasting to everlasting
the LORD's love is with those who fear him.

Psalm 103:17

The LORD your God is with you,
    he is mighty to save.
He will take great delight in you,
    he will quiet you with his love,
    he will rejoice over you with singing.

Zephaniah 3:17

❧

"My Presence goes with you," says the LORD, "and I will give you rest."

Exodus 33:14

Jesus said, "Peace I leave with you; my peace I give you. I do not give to you as the world gives. Do not let your hearts be troubled and do not be afraid."

John 14:27

❧

God is our refuge and strength,
    an ever-present help in trouble.
Therefore we will not fear, though
    the earth give way
and the mountains fall
    into the heart of the sea. . . .
The LORD Almighty is with us.

Psalm 46:1–2, 7

We ... rejoice in our sufferings, because we know that suffering produces perseverance; perseverance, character; and character, hope. And hope does not disappoint us, because God has poured out his love into our hearts by the Holy Spirit, whom he has given us.

Romans 5:3–5

May the Lord direct your hearts into God's love
and Christ's perseverance.

2 Thessalonians 3:5

❧

Surely goodness and love will follow me
    all the days of my life,
and I will dwell in the house of the LORD
        forever.

Psalm 23:6

May our Lord Jesus Christ himself and God our Father, who loved us and by his grace gave us eternal encouragement and good hope, encourage your hearts and strengthen you in every good deed and word.

2 Thessalonians 2:16–17

Those who hope in the LORD
     will renew their strength.
They will soar on wings like eagles;
          they will run and not grow weary,
          they will walk and not be faint.

Isaiah 40:31

*"B*ecause he loves me," says the LORD, "I will
rescue him;
I will protect him, for he acknowledges my name.
He will call upon me, and I will answer him;
I will be with him in trouble,
I will deliver him and honor him.
With long life will I satisfy him
and show him my salvation."

Psalm 91:14–16

$\mathcal{B}$ecause the Sovereign LORD helps me,
    I will not be disgraced.
Therefore have I set my face like flint,
    and I know I will not be put to shame.

Isaiah 50:7

❧

$\mathcal{W}$ho shall separate us from the love of Christ? Shall trouble or hardship or persecution? . . . No, in all these things we are more than conquerors through him who loved us.

Romans 8:35, 37

One thing I do: Forgetting what is behind and straining toward what is ahead, I press on toward the goal to win the prize for which God has called me heavenward in Christ Jesus.

Philippians 3:13–14

$\mathcal{L}$et your face shine on your servant, O LORD;
    save me in your unfailing love.

Psalm 31:16

❧

"$\mathcal{I}$ am with you and will watch over you wherever
you go. . . . I will not leave you until I have done
what I have promised you," says the LORD.

Genesis 28:15

GOD'S DEEP
LOVE

The angel of the LORD encamps around those
      who fear him,
      and he delivers them.
Taste and see that the LORD is good;
      blessed is the man who takes refuge in him.
Fear the LORD, you his saints,
      for those who fear him lack nothing.
The lions may grow weak and hungry,
      but those who seek the LORD lack no good
      thing.

Psalm 34:7–10

*Y*ou save the humble
  but bring low those whose eyes are haughty.
You, O LORD, keep my lamp burning;
  my God turns my darkness into light.
With your help I can advance against a troop;
  with my God I can scale a wall.
As for God, his way is perfect;
  the word of the LORD is flawless.
He is a shield
  for all who take refuge in him.

Psalm 18:27–30

How great is the love the Father has lavished on us, that we should be called children of God! And that is what we are!

1 John 3:1

God so loved the world that he gave his one and only Son, that whoever believes in him shall not perish but have eternal life. For God did not send his Son into the world to condemn the world, but to save the world through him.

John 3:16–17

*T*he LORD gives strength to his people;
    the LORD blesses his people with peace.
> *Psalm 29:11*

❧

*L*ove covers over all wrongs.
> *Proverbs 10:12*

❧

*B*y day the LORD directs his love,
    at night his song is with me—
    a prayer to the God of my life.
> *Psalm 42:8*

Jesus said, "He who loves me will be loved by my Father, and I too will love him and show myself to him."

John 14:21

❧

The LORD tends his flock like a shepherd:
He gathers the lambs in his arms
and carries them close to his heart;
he gently leads those that have young.

Isaiah 40:11

No eye has seen, no ear has heard, no mind has conceived what God has prepared for those who love him.

1 Corinthians 2:9

❧

John wrote, "I heard a loud voice from the throne saying, 'Now the dwelling of God is with men, and he will live with them. They will be his people, and God himself will be with them and be their God. He will wipe every tear from their eyes. There will be no more death or mourning or crying or pain, for the old order of things has passed away.' He who was seated on the throne said, 'I am making everything new!'"

Revelation 21:3–5

Love is patient, love is kind. It does not envy, it does not boast, it is not proud. It is not rude, it is not self-seeking, it is not easily angered, it keeps no record of wrongs.

1 Corinthians 13:4–5

This is what the LORD says—
 he who created you, . . .
"Fear not, for I have redeemed you;
I have summoned you by name; you are mine."

Isaiah 43:1

Show us your unfailing love, O LORD,
 and grant us your salvation.

Psalm 85:7

I pray that out of God's glorious riches he may strengthen you with power through his Spirit in your inner being, so that Christ may dwell in your hearts through faith. And I pray that you, being rooted and established in love, may have power, together with all the saints, to grasp how wide and long and high and deep is the love of Christ, and to know this love that surpasses knowledge—that you may be filled to the measure of all the fullness of God.

Ephesians 3:16–19

When I consider your heavens,
    the work of your fingers,
the moon and the stars,
    which you have set in place,
what is man that you are mindful of him,
    the son of man that you care for him?
You made him a little lower than the heavenly beings
    and crowned him with glory and honor.
You made him ruler over the works of your hands;
    you put everything under his feet:
all flocks and herds,
    and the beasts of the field,
the birds of the air,
    and the fish of the sea,
    all that swim the paths of the seas.
O LORD, our LORD,
    how majestic is your name in all the earth!

Psalm 8:3–9

May your unfailing love rest upon us, O LORD,
even as we put our hope in you.

Psalm 33:22

❧

O LORD, you bless the righteous;
you surround them with your favor as with
a shield.

Psalm 5:12

Let us love one another, for love comes from God. Everyone who loves has been born of God and knows God. Whoever does not love does not know God, because God is love. This is how God showed his love among us: He sent his one and only Son into the world that we might live through him. This is love: not that we loved God, but that he loved us and sent his Son as an atoning sacrifice for our sins. Dear friends, since God so loved us, we also ought to love one another. No one has ever seen God; but if we love one another, God lives in us and his love is made complete in us.

1 John 4:7–12

The LORD is good,
    a refuge in times of trouble.
He cares for those who trust in him.

Nahum 1:7

❧

You are forgiving and good, O LORD,
    abounding in love to all who call to you.

Psalm 86:5

❧

I love the LORD, for he heard my voice;
    he heard my cry for mercy.
Because he turned his ear to me,
    I will call on him as long as I live.

Psalm 116:1–2

Jesus said, "Come to me, all you who are weary and burdened, and I will give you rest. Take my yoke upon you and learn from me, for I am gentle and humble in heart, and you will find rest for your souls. For my yoke is easy and my burden is light."

Matthew 11:28–30

When the kindness and love of God our Savior appeared, he saved us, not because of righteous things we had done, but because of his mercy. He saved us through the washing of rebirth and renewal by the Holy Spirit, whom he poured out on us generously through Jesus Christ our Savior, so that, having been justified by his grace, we might become heirs having the hope of eternal life.

Titus 3:4–7

The LORD delights in those who fear him,
who put their hope in his unfailing love.

Psalm 147:11

❧

We do not have a high priest who is unable to
sympathize with our weaknesses, but we have one
who has been tempted in every way, just as we are—
yet was without sin. Let us then approach the throne
of grace with confidence, so that we may receive
mercy and find grace to help us in our time of need.

Hebrews 4:15–16

THE GIFT OF A
LOVING
FRIENDSHIP

There is a friend who sticks closer than a brother.

Proverbs 18:24

❧

Two are better than one,
    because they have a good return for their work:
If one falls down,
    his friend can help him up.
But pity the man who falls
    and has no one to help him up!
Also, if two lie down together, they will keep warm.
    But how can one keep warm alone?
Though one may be overpowered,
    two can defend themselves.
A cord of three strands is not quickly broken.

Ecclesiastes 4:9–12

*W*ounds from a friend can be trusted.

Proverbs 27:6

❧

*I*f we walk in the light, as Christ is in the light,
we have fellowship with one another.

1 John 1:7

$\mathcal{J}$esus said, "Greater love has no one than this, that he lay down his life for his friends. You are my friends if you do what I command. I no longer call you servants, because a servant does not know his master's business. Instead, I have called you friends."

John 15:13–15

*P*erfume and incense bring joy to the heart,
   and the pleasantness of one's friend springs
   from his earnest counsel.

Proverbs 27:9

❧

*B*e devoted to one another in brotherly love.
Honor one another above yourselves.

Romans 12:10

❧

*M*y intercessor is my friend
   as my eyes pour out tears to God.

Job 16:20

$\mathcal{B}$e completely humble and gentle; be patient, bearing with one another in love. Make every effort to keep the unity of the Spirit through the bond of peace.

Ephesians 4:2–3

$\mathcal{A}$ friend loves at all times,
and a brother is born for adversity.

Proverbs 17:17

LOVING
WORDS

May the words of my mouth
   and the meditation of my heart
   be pleasing in your sight, O LORD.
   Psalm 19:14

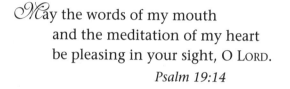

The tongue that brings healing is a tree of life.
   Proverbs 15:4

From the fruit of his lips a man enjoys good
   things.

Proverbs 13:2

❧

Confess your sins to each other and pray for
each other so that you may be healed.

James 5:16

❧

The mouth of the righteous man utters wisdom,
   and his tongue speaks what is just.
The law of his God is in his heart;
   his feet do not slip.

Psalm 37:30–31

Jesus said, "The good man brings good things out of the good stored up in his heart. . . . For out of the overflow of his heart his mouth speaks."

Luke 6:45

❧

If anyone speaks, he should do it as one speaking the very words of God.

1 Peter 4:11

*S*peak to one another with psalms, hymns and spiritual songs. Sing and make music in your heart to the Lord, always giving thanks to God the Father for everything, in the name of our Lord Jesus Christ.

Ephesians 5:19–20

❧

*T*hrough Jesus ... let us continually offer to God a sacrifice of praise—the fruit of lips that confess his name.

Hebrews 13:15

❧

A word aptly spoken
    is like apples of gold in settings of silver.

Proverbs 25:11

Pleasant words are a honeycomb,
sweet to the soul and healing to the bones.

Proverbs 16:24

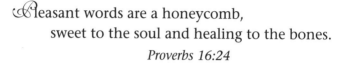

It is with your heart that you believe and are
justified, and it is with your mouth that you confess
and are saved.

Romans 10:10

$\mathcal{L}$ORD, who may dwell in your sanctuary?
        Who may live on your holy hill?
He whose walk is blameless
        and who does what is righteous,
who speaks the truth from his heart.

Psalm 15:1–2

❧

Jesus said, "The words I have spoken to you are spirit and they are life."

John 6:63

❧

$\mathcal{T}$he Sovereign LORD has given me
        an instructed tongue,
to know the word that sustains the weary.

Isaiah 50:4

A man finds joy in giving an apt reply—
and how good is a timely word!

Proverbs 15:23

❧

The Lord himself will come down from heaven,
with a loud command, with the voice of the
archangel and with the trumpet call of God, and . . .
we who are still alive and are left will be caught up
together with them in the clouds to meet the Lord in
the air. And so we will be with the Lord forever.
Therefore encourage each other with these words.

1 Thessalonians 4:16–18

We have different gifts, according to the grace given us. If a man's gift is prophesying, let him use it in proportion to his faith. If it is serving, let him serve; if it is teaching, let him teach; if it is encouraging, let him encourage.

Romans 12:6–8

❧

Faith comes from hearing the message, and the message is heard through the word of Christ.

Romans 10:17

❧

The words of the LORD are flawless,
   like silver refined in a furnace of clay,
   purified seven times.

Psalm 12:6

The Spirit helps us in our weakness. We do not know what we ought to pray for, but the Spirit himself intercedes for us with groans that words cannot express.

Romans 8:26

❧

Listen, O heavens, and I will speak;
    hear, O earth, the words of my mouth.
Let my teaching fall like rain
    and my words descend like dew,
like showers on new grass,
    like abundant rain on tender plants.
I will proclaim the name of the LORD.
    Oh, praise the greatness of our God!

Deuteronomy 32:1–3

Always be prepared to give an answer to everyone who asks you to give the reason for the hope that you have. But do this with gentleness and respect, keeping a clear conscience.

1 Peter 3:15–16

❧

My words come from an upright heart;
    my lips sincerely speak what I know.
The Spirit of God has made me;
    the breath of the Almighty gives me life.

Job 33:3–4

My tongue will speak of your righteousness
and of your praises all day long, O LORD.

Psalm 35:28

❧

Encourage one another daily.

Hebrews 3:13

❧

Speaking the truth in love, we will in all things
grow up into him who is the Head, that is, Christ.

Ephesians 4:15

*M*any, O Lord my God,
   are the wonders you have done.
The things you planned for us
   no one can recount to you;
were I to speak and tell of them,
   they would be too many to declare.

Psalm 40:5

$\mathcal{L}$et your conversation be always full of grace, seasoned with salt, so that you may know how to answer everyone.

Colossians 4:6

$\mathcal{L}$

$\mathcal{T}$he tongue of the righteous is choice silver.

Proverbs 10:20

FAITHFUL LOVE

*Y*our love, O LORD, reaches to the heavens,
   your faithfulness to the skies.

Psalm 36:5

❧

I sought the LORD, and he answered me;
   he delivered me from all my fears.
Those who look to him are radiant;
   their faces are never covered with shame.

Psalm 34:4–5

I, the LORD, will betroth you to me forever;
  I will betroth you
    in righteousness and justice,
    in love and compassion.
I will betroth you in faithfulness,
  and you will acknowledge the LORD.

Hosea 2:19–20

❧

*Y*our word, O LORD, is eternal;
  it stands firm in the heavens.

Psalm 119:89

The LORD is good and his love endures forever;
  his faithfulness continues
  through all generations.

Psalm 100:5

❧

Commit your way to the LORD;
  trust in him and he will do this:
He will make your righteousness shine like the dawn,
  the justice of your cause like the noonday sun.

Psalm 37:5–6

"Though the mountains be shaken
    and the hills be removed,
yet my unfailing love for you will not be shaken
    nor my covenant of peace be removed,"
    says the LORD, who has compassion on you.

Isaiah 54:10

❧

God who began a good work in you will carry it
on to completion until the day of Christ Jesus.

Philippians 1:6

God is our refuge and strength,
    an ever-present help in trouble.
Therefore we will not fear, though the earth give way
    and the mountains fall
    into the heart of the sea,
though its waters roar and foam
    and the mountains quake with their surging.

Psalm 46:1–3

Let us hold unswervingly to the hope we profess, for God who promised is faithful.

Hebrews 10:23

❧

The LORD, the LORD, the compassionate and gracious God, slow to anger, abounding in love and faithfulness.

Exodus 34:6

❧

The LORD loves the just
    and will not forsake his faithful ones.
They will be protected forever.

Psalm 37:28

The LORD your God goes with you; he will never leave you nor forsake you.

Deuteronomy 31:6

❧

The word of the LORD is right and true;
	he is faithful in all he does.
The LORD loves righteousness and justice;
	the earth is full of his unfailing love.

Psalm 33:4–5

The Lord is faithful, and he will strengthen and protect you from the evil one.

2 Thessalonians 3:3

❧

Have mercy on me, O God,
		according to your unfailing love;
according to your great compassion
		blot out my transgressions.

Psalm 51:1

❧

The Lord's unfailing love
		surrounds the man who trusts in him.

Psalm 32:10

"Can a mother forget the baby at her breast
    and have no compassion
    on the child she has borne?
Though she may forget,
    I will not forget you!
See, I have engraved you on the palms of my hands;
    your walls are ever before me,"
        declares the LORD.

Isaiah 49:15–16

The LORD your God is a merciful God; he will
not abandon or destroy you or forget the
covenant with your forefathers.

Deuteronomy 4:31

❧

Jesus said, "Remain in me, and I will remain in
you."

John 15:4

❧

All the ways of the LORD are loving and faithful
  for those who keep
  the demands of his covenant.

Psalm 25:10

$\mathcal{I}$ am convinced that neither death nor life, neither angels nor demons, neither the present nor the future, nor any powers, neither height nor depth, nor anything else in all creation, will be able to separate us from the love of God that is in Christ Jesus our Lord.

Romans 8:38–39

❧

$\mathcal{C}$ontinue your love to those
    who know you, O LORD,
        your righteousness to the upright in heart.

Psalm 36:10

*Y*ou hem me in—behind and before, O LORD;
   you have laid your hand upon me.
Such knowledge is too wonderful for me,
   too lofty for me to attain.
Where can I go from your Spirit?
   Where can I flee from your presence?
If I go up to the heavens, you are there;
   if I make my bed in the depths,
      you are there.
If I rise on the wings of the dawn,
   if I settle on the far side of the sea,
even there your hand will guide me,
   your right hand will hold me fast.

Psalm 139:5–10

$\mathcal{B}$e strong and courageous. Do not be terrified; do not be discouraged, for the LORD your God will be with you wherever you go.

Joshua 1:9

❧

$\mathcal{T}$he LORD is gracious and righteous;
　　our God is full of compassion.
The LORD protects the simplehearted;
　　when I was in great need, he saved me.
Be at rest once more, O my soul,
　　for the LORD has been good to you.

Psalm 116:5–7

$\mathcal{J}$esus said, "I will not leave you as orphans; I will come to you."

John 14:18

❧

$\mathcal{L}$et the morning bring me word of your
    unfailing love,
    for I have put my trust in you.
Show me the way I should go,
    for to you I lift up my soul.

Psalm 143:8

Praise the LORD, all you nations;
    extol him, all you peoples.
For great is his love toward us,
    and the faithfulness of the LORD
    endures forever.
Praise the LORD.

Psalm 117:1–2

❧

Jesus said, "Surely I am with you always, to the very end of the age."

Matthew 28:20

*J*esus said, "If you obey my commands, you will remain in my love, just as I have obeyed my Father's commands and remain in his love. I have told you this so that my joy may be in you and that your joy may be complete."

John 15:10–11

❧

*T*o him who is able to keep you from falling and to present you before his glorious presence without fault and with great joy—to the only God our Savior be glory, majesty, power and authority, through Jesus Christ our Lord, before all ages, now and forevermore! Amen.

Jude 24–25

You also were included in Christ when you heard the word of truth, the gospel of your salvation. Having believed, you were marked in him with a seal, the promised Holy Spirit, who is a deposit guaranteeing our inheritance until the redemption of those who are God's possession—to the praise of his glory.

Ephesians 1:13–14

❧

God will keep you strong to the end, so that you will be blameless on the day of our Lord Jesus Christ. God, who has called you into fellowship with his Son Jesus Christ our Lord, is faithful.

1 Corinthians 1:8–9

This I call to mind
    and therefore I have hope:
Because of the LORD's great love we are not
    consumed,
    for his compassions never fail.
They are new every morning;
    great is your faithfulness.

Lamentations 3:21–23

$\mathcal{J}$esus said, "Well done, good and faithful servant! You have been faithful with a few things; I will put you in charge of many things. Come and share your master's happiness!"

Matthew 25:21

❧

$\mathcal{G}$od will cover you with his feathers,
and under his wings you will find refuge;
his faithfulness will be your shield and rampart.

Psalm 91:4

God sends his love and his faithfulness. . . .
I will praise you, O LORD, among the nations;
    I will sing of you among the peoples.
For great is your love, reaching to the heavens;
    your faithfulness reaches to the skies.

Psalm 57:3, 9–10

The fruit of the Spirit is love, joy, peace, patience, kindness, goodness, faithfulness, gentleness and self-control.

Galatians 5:22–23

❧

Jesus said, "My sheep listen to my voice; I know them, and they follow me. I give them eternal life, and they shall never perish; no one can snatch them out of my hand. My Father, who has given them to me, is greater than all; no one can snatch them out of my Father's hand. I and the Father are one."

John 10:27–30

LOVING
OTHERS

Carry each other's burdens, and in this way you will fulfill the law of Christ.

Galatians 6:2

❧

Jesus said, "Love one another. As I have loved you, so you must love one another. By this all men will know that you are my disciples, if you love one another."

John 13:34–35

$\mathcal{D}$o not forget to do good and to share with others, for with such sacrifices God is pleased.

Hebrews 13:16

❧

$\mathcal{W}$e continually remember before our God and Father your work produced by faith, your labor prompted by love, and your endurance inspired by hope in our Lord Jesus Christ.

1 Thessalonians 1:3

"Is not this the kind of fasting I have chosen:
to loose the chains of injustice
    and untie the cords of the yoke,
to set the oppressed free
    and break every yoke?
Is it not to share your food with the hungry
    and to provide the poor wanderer with
    shelter . . .
Then your light will break forth like the dawn,
    and your healing will quickly appear;
then your righteousness will go before you,
    and the glory of the LORD
    will be your rear guard.
Then you will call, and the LORD will answer;
    you will cry for help, and he will say:
    Here am I," declares the LORD.

Isaiah 58:6–9

Love is patient, love is kind. It does not envy, it does not boast, it is not proud. It is not rude, it is not self-seeking, it is not easily angered, it keeps no record of wrongs. Love does not delight in evil but rejoices with the truth. It always protects, always trusts, always hopes, always perseveres. Love never fails.

1 Corinthians 13:4–8

Jesus said, "When you give a banquet, invite the poor, the crippled, the lame, the blind, and you will be blessed. Although they cannot repay you, you will be repaid at the resurrection of the righteous."

Luke 14:13–14

❧

Love the Lord your God with all your heart and with all your soul and with all your mind and with all your strength. . . . Love your neighbor as yourself. There is no commandment greater than these.

Mark 12:30–31

*H*e who refreshes others will himself be
refreshed.

Proverbs 11:25

❧

A kindhearted woman gains respect.

Proverbs 11:16

❧

*J*esus said, "Love your enemies, do good to
them, and lend to them without expecting to get
anything back. Then your reward will be great."

Luke 6:35

*M*any women were [at the crucifixion], watching from a distance. They had followed Jesus from Galilee to care for his needs. Among them were Mary Magdalene, Mary the mother of James and Joses, and the mother of Zebedee's sons.

Matthew 27:55–56

❧

*J*ust as each of us has one body with many members, and these members do not all have the same function, so in Christ we who are many form one body, and each member belongs to all the others.

Romans 12:4–5

"If you spend yourselves in behalf of the
hungry
and satisfy the needs of the oppressed,
then your light will rise in the darkness,
and your night will become like the
noonday.
The LORD will guide you always;
he will satisfy your needs in a sun-scorched
land
and will strengthen your frame.
You will be like a well-watered garden,
like a spring whose waters never fail," says
the LORD.

Isaiah 58:10–11

$\mathcal{J}$esus said, "Love your enemies and pray for those who persecute you, that you may be sons of your Father in heaven."

Matthew 5:44–45

$\mathcal{A}$ll of you, live in harmony with one another; be sympathetic, love, . . . be compassionate and humble. Do not repay evil with evil or insult with insult, but with blessing, because to this you were called so that you may inherit a blessing.

1 Peter 3:8–9

*Y*ou will be made rich in every way so that you can be generous on every occasion, and . . . your generosity will result in thanksgiving to God.

2 Corinthians 9:11

❧

*G*ood will come to him who is generous and
    lends freely,
        who conducts his affairs with justice.

Psalm 112:5

❧

*E*ach of you should look not only to your own interests, but also to the interests of others. Your attitude should be the same as that of Christ Jesus.

Philippians 2:4–5

*W*hoever loves his brother lives in the light, and there is nothing in him to make him stumble.

1 John 2:10

*D*o to others as you would have them do to you.

Luke 6:31

GOD'S LOVING FORGIVENESS

If we confess our sins, God is faithful and just and will forgive us our sins and purify us from all unrighteousness.

1 John 1:9

❧

I acknowledged my sin to you, O LORD,
and did not cover up my iniquity.
I said, "I will confess
my transgressions to the LORD"—
and you forgave
the guilt of my sin.

Psalm 32:5

Blessed is he
> whose transgressions are forgiven,
> whose sins are covered.
Blessed is the man
> whose sin the LORD
> does not count against him
> and in whose spirit is no deceit.

Psalm 32:1–2

❦

"If my people, who are called by my name, will humble themselves and pray and seek my face and turn from their wicked ways, then will I hear from heaven and will forgive their sin and will heal their land," declares the LORD.

2 Chronicles 7:14

Jesus said, "I tell you the truth, whoever hears my word and believes him who sent me has eternal life and will not be condemned; he has crossed over from death to life."

John 5:24

❧

God made Christ who had no sin to be sin for us, so that in him we might become the righteousness of God.

2 Corinthians 5:21

"Come now, let us reason together,"
    says the LORD.
"Though your sins are like scarlet,
    they shall be as white as snow;
though they are red as crimson,
    they shall be like wool."

Isaiah 1:18

The grace of God that brings salvation has appeared to all men. It teaches us to say "No" to ungodliness and worldly passions, and to live self-controlled, upright and godly lives in this present age, while we wait for the blessed hope—the glorious appearing of our great God and Savior, Jesus Christ, who gave himself for us to redeem us from all wickedness and to purify for himself a people that are his very own, eager to do what is good.

Titus 2:11–14

*W*ho is a God like you,
    who pardons sin and forgives the
        transgression
    of the remnant of his inheritance?
You do not stay angry forever
    but delight to show mercy.
You will again have compassion on us;
    you will tread our sins underfoot
    and hurl all our iniquities
    into the depths of the sea.

Micah 7:18–19

$\mathcal{N}$ow in Christ Jesus you who once were far away have been brought near through the blood of Christ. For he himself is our peace, who has made the two one and has destroyed the barrier, the dividing wall of hostility.

Ephesians 2:13–14

❧

"$\mathcal{I}$, even I, am he who blots out
    your transgressions, for my own sake,
    and remembers your sins no more," says the
    LORD.

Isaiah 43:25

As high as the heavens are above the earth,
    so great is God's love for those
    who fear him;
as far as the east is from the west,
    so far has he removed our transgressions
        from us.
As a father has compassion on his children,
    so the LORD has compassion on those who
        fear him;
for he knows how we are formed,
    he remembers that we are dust.

Psalm 103:11–14

If anyone is in Christ, he is a new creation; the old has gone, the new has come!

2 Corinthians 5:17

❧

There is now no condemnation for those who are in Christ Jesus, because through Christ Jesus the law of the Spirit of life set me free from the law of sin and death.

Romans 8:1–2

GOD'S LOVING PROVISION

$\mathcal{D}$o not be anxious about anything, but in everything, by prayer and petition, with thanksgiving, present your requests to God. And the peace of God, which transcends all understanding, will guard your hearts and your minds in Christ Jesus.

Philippians 4:6–7

❧

$\mathcal{T}$he LORD upholds all those who fall
    and lifts up all who are bowed down.
The eyes of all look to you,
    and you give them their food
    at the proper time.
You open your hand
    and satisfy the desires of every living thing.
The LORD is righteous in all his ways
    and loving toward all he has made.

Psalm 145:14–17

God who did not spare his own Son, but gave him up for us all—how will he not also, along with him, graciously give us all things?

Romans 8:32

❧

A righteous man may have many troubles, but the LORD delivers him from them all.

Psalm 34:19

I was young and now I am old,
    yet I have never seen the righteous forsaken
    or their children begging bread.
They are always generous and lend freely;
    their children will be blessed.

Psalm 37:25–26

This poor man called, and the LORD heard him;
    he saved him out of all his troubles.

Psalm 34:6

Jesus said, "Whatever you ask for in prayer, believe that you have received it, and it will be yours."

Mark 11:24

❧

God is able to make all grace abound to you, so that in all things at all times, having all that you need, you will abound in every good work.

2 Corinthians 9:8

❧

Just as the sufferings of Christ flow over into our lives, so also through Christ our comfort overflows.

2 Corinthians 1:5

Jesus said, "Do not worry about your life, what you will eat or drink; or about your body, what you will wear. Is not life more important than food, and the body more important than clothes? Look at the birds of the air; they do not sow or reap or store away in barns, and yet your heavenly Father feeds them. Are you not much more valuable than they?"

Matthew 6:25–26

God who supplies seed to the sower and bread for food will also supply and increase your store of seed and will enlarge the harvest of your righteousness.

2 Corinthians 9:10

❧

Trust in the LORD and do good;
    dwell in the land and enjoy safe pasture.

Psalm 37:3

*T*hey cried out to the Lord in their trouble,
and he delivered them from their distress.
He led them by a straight way
to a city where they could settle.
Let them give thanks to the Lord
for his unfailing love
and his wonderful deeds for men,
for he satisfies the thirsty
and fills the hungry with good things.

Psalm 107:6–9

$\mathcal{C}$ast all your anxiety on God because he cares for you.

1 Peter 5:7

❧

"$\mathcal{B}$ring the whole tithe into the storehouse, that there may be food in my house. Test me in this," says the LORD Almighty, "and see if I will not throw open the floodgates of heaven and pour out so much blessing that you will not have room enough for it."

Malachi 3:10

Jesus said, "Do not worry, saying, 'What shall we eat?' or 'What shall we drink?' or 'What shall we wear?' For the pagans run after all these things, and your heavenly Father knows that you need them. But seek first his kingdom and his righteousness, and all these things will be given to you as well. Therefore do not worry about tomorrow, for tomorrow will worry about itself. Each day has enough trouble of its own."

Matthew 6:31–34

*W*hoever trusts in the L<small>ORD</small> is kept safe.

Proverbs 29:25

❧

*G*od has said, "Never will I leave you; never will I forsake you." So we say with confidence, "The Lord is my helper; I will not be afraid. What can man do to me?"

Hebrews 13:5–6

God will meet all your needs according to his glorious riches in Christ Jesus.

Philippians 4:19

❧

I have learned to be content whatever the circumstances. I know what it is to be in need, and I know what it is to have plenty. I have learned the secret of being content in any and every situation, whether well fed or hungry, whether living in plenty or in want. I can do everything through Christ who gives me strength.

Philippians 4:11–13

*H*as not God chosen those who are poor in the eyes of the world to be rich in faith and to inherit the kingdom he promised those who love him?

James 2:5

❧

*J*esus said, "I tell you the truth, my Father will give you whatever you ask in my name. Until now you have not asked for anything in my name. Ask and you will receive, and your joy will be complete."

John 16:23–24

The days of the blameless are known to the LORD,
   and their inheritance will endure forever.
In times of disaster they will not wither;
   in days of famine they will enjoy plenty.

Psalm 37:18–19

❧

The LORD longs to be gracious to you;
   he rises to show you compassion.
For the LORD is a God of justice.
   Blessed are all who wait for him!

Isaiah 30:18

LOVING GOD THROUGH WORSHIP

Jesus said, "A time is coming and has now come when the true worshipers will worship the Father in spirit and truth, for they are the kind of worshipers the Father seeks. God is spirit, and his worshipers must worship in spirit and in truth."

John 4:23–24

❧

O LORD, I trust in your unfailing love;
    my heart rejoices in your salvation.
I will sing to the LORD,
    for he has been good to me.

Psalm 13:5–6

❧

You are a chosen people, a royal priesthood, a holy nation, a people belonging to God, that you may declare the praises of him who called you out of darkness into his wonderful light.

1 Peter 2:9

The LORD is exalted over all the nations,
    his glory above the heavens.
Who is like the LORD our God,
    the One who sits enthroned on high,
who stoops down to look
    on the heavens and the earth?
He raises the poor from the dust
    and lifts the needy from the ash heap;
he seats them with princes,
    with the princes of their people.
He settles the barren woman in her home
    as a happy mother of children.
Praise the LORD.

Psalm 113:4–9

Jesus said, "I tell you that if two of you on earth agree about anything you ask for, it will be done for you by my Father in heaven. For where two or three come together in my name, there am I with them."

Matthew 18:19–20

❧

Sing to the LORD a new song,
    his praise in the assembly of the saints.
Let Israel rejoice in their Maker;
    let the people of Zion be glad in their King.
Let them praise his name with dancing
    and make music to him
    with tambourine and harp.
For the LORD takes delight in his people;
    he crowns the humble with salvation.

Psalm 149:1–4

$\mathcal{O}$ God, you are my God,
 earnestly I seek you;
my soul thirsts for you,
 my body longs for you,
in a dry and weary land
 where there is no water.
I have seen you in the sanctuary
 and beheld your power and your glory.
Because your love is better than life,
 my lips will glorify you.
I will praise you as long as I live,
 and in your name I will lift up my hands.
My soul will be satisfied as with
 the richest of foods;
  with singing lips my mouth will praise you.

Psalm 63:1–5

They raised their voices in praise to the LORD and sang: "He is good; his love endures forever." Then the temple of the LORD was filled with a cloud, and the priests could not perform their service because of the cloud, for the glory of the LORD filled the temple of God.

2 Chronicles 5:13–14

❧

Give thanks to the LORD, for he is good;
    his love endures forever.

Psalm 106:1

❧

Sing joyfully to the LORD, you righteous;
    it is fitting for the upright to praise him.

Psalm 33:1

One thing I ask of the LORD,
     this is what I seek:
that I may dwell in the house of the LORD
     all the days of my life,
to gaze upon the beauty of the LORD
     and to seek him in his temple.
For in the day of trouble
     he will keep me safe in his dwelling;
he will hide me in the shelter of his tabernacle
     and set me high upon a rock.
Then my head will be exalted
     above the enemies who surround me;
at his tabernacle will I sacrifice with shouts of joy;
     I will sing and make music to the LORD.

Psalm 27:4–6

"He who sacrifices thank offerings honors me,"
   says the LORD,
   "and he prepares the way
   so that I may show him the salvation of God."

Psalm 50:23

❧

Rejoice in the Lord always. I will say it again:
Rejoice!

Philippians 4:4

Come, let us bow down in worship,
	let us kneel before the LORD our Maker;
for he is our God
	and we are the people of his pasture,
	the flock under his care.

Psalm 95:6–7

❧

O LORD, I call to you; come quickly to me.
	Hear my voice when I call to you.
May my prayer be set before you like incense;
	may the lifting up of my hands be like the
	evening sacrifice.

Psalm 141:1–2

*H*ow beautiful on the mountains
>   are the feet of those who bring good news,
who proclaim peace,
>   who bring good tidings,
>   who proclaim salvation,
who say to Zion,
>   "Your God reigns!"
Listen! Your watchmen lift up their voices;
>   together they shout for joy.
When the LORD returns to Zion,
>   they will see it with their own eyes.
Burst into songs of joy together,
>   you ruins of Jerusalem,
for the LORD has comforted his people,
>   he has redeemed Jerusalem.

Isaiah 52:7–9

How can I repay the LORD
for all his goodness to me?
I will lift up the cup of salvation
and call on the name of the LORD.
I will fulfill my vows to the LORD
in the presence of all his people.

Psalm 116:12–14

❧

It is good to praise the LORD
and make music to your name, O Most High,
to proclaim your love in the morning
and your faithfulness at night,
to the music of the ten-stringed lyre
and the melody of the harp.
For you make me glad by your deeds, O LORD;
I sing for joy at the works of your hands.
How great are your works, O LORD,
how profound your thoughts!

Psalm 92:1–5

Praise the LORD, O my soul;
     all my inmost being, praise his holy name.
Praise the LORD, O my soul,
     and forget not all his benefits—
who forgives all your sins
     and heals all your diseases,
who redeems your life from the pit
     and crowns you with love and compassion,
who satisfies your desires with good things
     so that your youth is renewed like the eagle's.

Psalm 103:1–5

❧

May the God who gives endurance and
encouragement give you a spirit of unity among
yourselves as you follow Christ Jesus, so that with
one heart and mouth you may glorify the God and
Father of our Lord Jesus Christ.

Romans 15:5–6